THE HOLYOKE

Also available in the series:

Eve Names the Animals by Susan Donnelly
Rain by William Carpenter
This Body of Silk by Sue Ellen Thompson
Valentino's Hair by Yvonne Sapia

The Morse Poetry Prize
Edited by Guy Rotella

FRANK GASPAR

The Holyoke

THE 1988 MORSE
POETRY PRIZE
SELECTED AND
INTRODUCED BY
MARY OLIVER

Northeastern University Press
BOSTON

Northeastern University Press

Library of Congress Cataloging in Publication Data

Gaspar, Frank, 1946–
    The holyoke / Frank Gaspar.
        p.   cm. — (The 1988 Morse Poetry Prize)
    ISBN 1-55553-039-7 (pbk. : alk. paper)
    I. Title. II. Series: Morse Poetry Prize : 1988.
    PS3557.A8448H.64   1988
    811'.54—dc19   88-21664
                                        CIP

Designed by Ann Twombly

Composed in Weiss by Eastern Typesetting Company,
South Windsor, Connecticut. Printed and bound by
some printer, some town, some state. The paper is
something, an acid-free sheet.

MANUFACTURED IN THE UNITED STATES OF AMERICA
93 92 91 90 89 88   5 4 3 2 1

For Georgia

ACKNOWLEDGMENTS

Poems in this book originally appeared in the following maga-zines: *Georgia Review* ("The Harbor in Winter"), *Kenyon Review* ("August," "Catechism," "Golden Colt Ranch," "Leaving Pico," "Passing," "Tia Joanna"), *Massachusetts Review* ("The Holyoke," "Waking"), *The Nation* ("Catwalk," "The Bullet Hole in the Twelfth-Street Door"), *New England Review and Bread Loaf Quarterly* ("Deer, Swimming" and "Silence," reprinted by permission of *New England Review and Bread Loaf Quarterly* 6, no. 2, Copyright © 1983 by Frank Gaspar), *Prairie Schooner* ("Answering," reprinted from *Prairie Schooner*, by permission of University of Nebraska Press, Copyright © 1983 by University of Nebraska Press), *Tightrope* ("Potatoes"), and *Wisconsin Review* ("The Old Country"). "The Har-bor in Winter" was reprinted in the *Anthology of Magazine Verse and Yearbook of American Poetry*, 1985.

Contents

PART THREE

Introduction

Frank Gaspar's poems are agile and forceful, their narratives are clear and absorbing, the collection does that difficult thing—it transcends its own total and becomes more than itself: *The Holyoke* is a distinguished book. A number of the manuscripts in this year's contest were both proficient and provocative. What brought me back time and again to *The Holyoke* was a sense that these poems *had* to be written, and that the language—inventive and careful or high-flying as it might be—was there only to be useful. Poems nowadays often address the reader with obvious insistence. "Let me tell you about my life," they say, "and I will make it fancy enough that you won't be bored." Frank Gaspar, I believe, has something else in mind. He is speaking to the reader—but also to himself, or perhaps to some hazy divinity, or to the blue sky. I felt in his voice no attempt to persuade me of anything. I felt only the abiding imperative to get it right. Which is, of course, what real writing is about.

The poems tell the old story: a young man's passage from boyhood to maturity, in a small town by the sea. His people are Portuguese and Catholic—fishermen, priests, a woman who once met St. Francis in the woods, a fishing captain who flies "the torn shirt / of his lost boy from the mizzen / of his dragger . . . ," a friend who "told us once in catechism / that he'd seen Jesus floating / in the dark sky, a soft light / above his house." In "Tia Joanna" we see

> the soft kerchiefs
> of the women, the dark cloth
> of their long coats, the kale cooking
> on the oilstoves in the redolent kitchens,
> the checkered shirts of the husbands,
> the fish they bring to the doorways when
>
> last light is fluttering in the eaves and cornices. . . .

At the heart of the book is the boy's quest—against the many voices of authority—for his own sense of some divine certainty. In Frank Gaspar's world this is not something you sit down and think about—it is something that arises directly out of humdrum, daily life, with its endless precarious situations. Significantly, a number of the poems are, on the first level, narratives about work. In the title poem, the author struggles to repair an old water heater:

> I spent the day there
> on the bathroom floor,
> measuring my way to the heart of the thing. . . .

"Diving for Money" and "Stealing Seed Clams from the Marsh" both bring in a little cash, but the greater triumph is the acceptance of such activities as experiences rather than necessary tasks. I believe this is called Grace.

It is also a world of questions that cannot be answered, or even asked. In the poem called "For No One," the writer points—without naming it—to an unsolvable sorrow:

> So in the scene they are picking berries:
> an old man, two women, the boy.
> It is the first time he understands the absence.

Teilhard de Chardin wrote that great sorrow is redemptive. Was it the absence of the father, perhaps, that taught Gaspar to be so fiercely attentive to the imperfect world? For this attention is the clue to his book. Frank Gaspar is attentive to everything. He is especially attentive to other lives. In "Ice Harvest," he describes his mother, who

> was only the girl
> in the corner of the photograph,
> a thin-faced kid, bundled
> in kerchief and coat,
> frozen stiff-shouldered,
> the look of all the rest
> of her life in her eyes.

Most of all he is attentive to what there is too much of—the dark-
ness. And he will not let it go until it gives up some glow, some
thrust of light—not nameable, not the body of Jesus seen by his
friend, but still a light brighter than the coins falling through the
water—more luminous than an easy life.

Because I have lived in Provincetown, Massachusetts, for many
years, it was impossible not to recognize the place-names of this
manuscript. Provincetown has been, and still is, a town where artists
and writers, Hans Hofmann among them, come to live and to work.
Over the years there has been a lot of talk about what the "creative"
people have added to the town—opinions voiced mainly by the
creative people themselves. Perhaps a sense of elitism is inevitable
in such a situation, perhaps not. None of us was born here. And
no one, if you get my meaning, ever considered the possibility of
a Frank Gaspar. That I was engaged by his work has nothing to do
with Provincetown but with the poems themselves, naturally. But
this part of the story, I decided, was also worth the telling.

MARY OLIVER

PART ONE

◢◤ Deer, Swimming

We were always among the first to know
when something worth any trouble happened,
like the time a live whale beached itself
behind the East End Cold Storage building,
or the time the captain of a Danish freighter
misread the channel lights
and ran his ship halfway to the parking lot
at Herring Cove,
so when we heard that one of the fishing boats
had caught a deer
we rode our bicycles to the end of the town wharf
with a cold west wind stinging our foreheads
and wet snow in our eyes.
We stood where the men talked
in the lee of the packing house,
where the boat bulled its heavy gunwales
into the wharf's pilings.
"Off Nantucket," someone said, "dragging for flounder
and here comes this deer swimming—
swimming, mind—miles out in those big swells."

The deer, a small doe, lay trussed on the deck,
still alive, a maroon stain at its mouth,
one bottomless eye staring up through the snow,
through the faces at the wharf's slick edge.
It would shudder from time to time
as if to knock the snow from its body,
but the snow clung, and we stood,
glad to be out of the wind,
until dusk yawned its wide, bleak yawn,
and the men sent us from the wharf.
We knew why.
An east-end kid, younger than we,

3

had died the winter before,
pinned beneath his bicycle in the shallow water.
Wind on our backs, we coasted down the wharf,
cautious on the treacherous planks,
although none of us took the men's warnings seriously.
Death was a curiosity
to pull us from the stuffy heat
of our houses on gray winter days.
Where did that deer think it was going,
think it could get to, swimming off like that?
By the time we reached the foot of the wharf,
the hard weather was becoming a real storm.
The town seemed to recede beneath it,
to move subtly away from us,
as if in deference, as our wheels spun
through the gathering snow.

The Harbor in Winter

The white harbor,
a mother's story or dream
given to us as a token of loss:
nothing could ever be that way again,
nothing ever quite so good, so
cold, so white. The picture
she gave us stood hard as a mirror
ringed in a heavy arm of snow,
and they came down, she said,
from the top of Franklin Hill
on double runners past the house
and wharf and out on that great ice,
skidding halfway to the weirs,
piled two and three on their brilliant sleds.

Like so much of what we wanted,
what we believed, it never was.
The slick, white hyperbole,
the purity of all that ice and snow,
the sound of runners trembling hard
on the thick harbor, the tide's pulse
brutally still under that bright table
all came from a woman's lips,
a voice hollowed to its own beliefs.

Nothing could ever be that way,
nothing. In my last year there
the weather came down from Canada,
and the pipes froze on a night in February.
I walked the harbor's edge and watched
the icy stars go out. The snow
came next, scudding white in the wharf's pale lamp,
and the harbor, harbor once

of glazed crystal, of dashing sleds,
of that woman's lilting story,
hissed under the winter sky,
swallowing light and sound.

ꗨ *Tia Joanna*

*"You are in God and God is in you
like the fish is in the sea and the sea
is in the fish"*   —St. Bernadette

When she enters the church, the mind
of God, though unknowable, becomes clear
as glass to her. His glory swims over her
the way the lights of the tiny fires swim
over the cylinders of the candles,
a particular light, an infinity
of small hearts that warm the world.

Everything is gathered here under the vaults,
within these heavy doors. She can look
deeply into the still face of the Mysteries
and smell the incense, the yellow blooms
coloring the air around the Virgin's head,
each black bead between her swollen fingers
telling lightly the rose of all her knowing.

And she knows then in the building's solemn space,
the creak of kneelers under her legs, the blurred
murmur of voices from the far confessional,
knows with an unshaking force that loss,
bounty, her fragile joy, *all there is* flows
easily from the placid mind of God,
and she can be touched by Him, indeed,

is touched by Him continually—she
is living in His body. The soft kerchiefs
of the women, the dark cloth
of their long coats, the kale cooking
on the oilstoves in the redolent kitchens,

7

the checkered shirts of the husbands,
the fish they bring to the doorways when

last light is fluttering in the eaves and cornices,
everything she can imagine in such
quiet and lucid moments as this, she sees
is contained in the mystery of His consuming presence.
It is dark when she finally leaves the church.
Yellow squares of light
mark the small windows of the houses:

She likes that, thinks of the host she will receive
in the morning, *His* light shining in her eyes.
But tonight still there is mackerel to pickle
with vinegar and garlic in the stone crock,
her husband's silver hair to trim, the bread
to set rising in the big china bowl
on the stool tucked close to the chimney.

Inside their house the world flattens and
constricts, the little rooms kneel to the statue
of the crucifixion, her husband sits at Christ's heels.
Tired from the boat and the day's work, he
barely greets her. His cough is growing deeper,
she thinks. She puts his scale-stuck boots
on the back steps. Go wash, she says in the old tongue.

Later, lying in the dark beside him she touches
the place where his ribs stop and the flesh is soft.
She is stunned sometimes by his softness.
He twitches in sleep, makes a sound like speech.
Shh, she whispers, and tightens her eyes.
She recalls how she has always understood
the things he cannot. She prays for him.

🍃 *Leaving Pico*

We heard *Pico* from the kitchen
where the living sat rolling
cigarettes in their thick fingers,
their bottles of Narragansett
in front of them on the table
where they sat and said *verde,*
green, like the backs
of certain fish or the throats
of the small birds that suck
at blossoms along the white-washed
fences in late spring:
green and clay roads, they said,
and the rolling walls
brushed white with lime,
and how many trunks
in the hold of a ship,
what dishes, what cloth, how many
rosaries and candles to the Virgin,
and the prayers for the old dead
they left to sleep under the wet hills
(the green hills, and at night
light from the oil lamps
and sometimes a guitar keening
and windmills that huddled white
over the small fields of the dead)
and all the time they were
preparing themselves behind
their violet lips and heavy eyes
to sleep in this different earth
consoled only by how the moon
and tide must set themselves
pulling off to other darkness
with as little notion of returning.

ᓴᐧ Potatoes

Potato patch: they come up
out of the ground like
gull's eggs or those
big ball bearings we call *hogs*.
By the fence kale does better,
long rows, green slugs
that smell like mint,
the mint itself anywhere
it pleases, wild and vagrant.
We feed it dishwater.
Yellowjackets orbit the
shaggy blossoms.

My brother hasn't come yet,
my stepfather hasn't come yet,
my great uncle sits in the canvas swing
in a straw hat. His hair
is thick and white. I lick
whisky from the edge
of his shotglass. *This
is what happens when you die,*
he says, holding his breath,
closing his eyes. Next door
in the feathery patch of anise
a blond cat stalks something.

*You need more ash in the ground
for those,* he says, old
man's finger unbending in the sun.
My mother holds the stunted potatoes
in a tin pot. Her look
is sullen and ashamed.
Nothing goes right for her. *You
can plant them next time,* she says.

He kicks the black dirt
with a heavy foot,
sets the swing going. He closes
his eyes, starts singing, singing.

ꙮ Ernestina the Shoemaker's Wife

"You have his eyes," she'd say to me,
and then to my old aunt, "Those are
the eyes I saw!" And she would tell again
how Saint Francis caught her in the woods
when she was a young girl. Dominic,

her husband, would never sit still
when she spoke of it, would rise slowly
from the Morris chair and go outside,
down the rows of kale and corn
to his barn, his hammers and lasts.

"He took the breath from under my heart,"
she said, her thin fingers crooked at her breast.
"It was not what you think. He was a power,
a beast. And the rain came down, and he held
me there, my dress sticking, my body showing."

When I wanted to wander out the door
and sit among the sharp-smelling *hervas*
in her garden, they let me go
and kept talking behind curtains
that breathed in and out in the slow air,

and they prayed the rosary together,
droning through the Mysteries. "Don't cross her,"
is what my mother said. "She's a *bruxa*
and can give you the evil eye herself."
"That kind of talk is foolish," said my aunt.

Whenever we left, my aunt would take
my arm and lean to me—"Remember
that she is only talking about a dream!"
But I remembered Dominic's hammering like a bell,
and how she said even the wet trees shivered.

✎ Beachcombing

We follow him on the beach,
slack tide, winter, no one
has begun to die yet. The salt-
rimmed heels of his workboots sink
into the wet sand. His step
is careful as he hunches over,
eyes the cold rubble. Our hands
are cold, fingers balled in our pockets.
Here, he says, stoops, pulls out a coin
from the darkness of shell and pebble,
an Indian Head growing green. My
brother takes it from his hand,
turns it quickly in his own stiff fingers,
gives it back. I find nothing
on these walks. The heaped flotsam
crackles under my wet shoes: skate eggs,
straw, squares of tarred net, bits of glass,
the dark scoops of mussel shells, pieces
of red brick smoothed by tide
trailing the bulbous seaweed that
on warmer days we squeeze and pop.
The wind can cut. He doesn't
feel it. He can find a mound
of rust that is a key, a square bottle
whole with letters on it, pieces
of clay pipes the old Yankees smoked
before our people ever came here.
His remarkable eyes. He can see
into another time when no one
has begun to die yet, kicks
at a piece of coal shining in a slick rill,
tells us how his old father made him
comb the beach for coal as a boy,

carry it home in a sack to dry
and burn. *You boys today,* he says.
He doesn't finish, stoops again
and picks up a pipe stem, white as bone,
holds it to the wind until
it whistles. *Do this just right
and the old dead men will talk to you.*
I wipe my nose
on the edge of my coatsleeve.
I can never tell when
he means what he is saying.

For No One

I know it was summer because of the berries,
berries on bushes, bushes crowding
an old road that ran to nothing
in purple woods, and light buzzing
and the soft heat rising like mist
from the trampled grass.
You were nowhere, nobody.

Grandfather was there, dressed
in a black coat. Maybe
it is a dream that I remember.
He was tired and sat eating
from his pail of berries.
I don't know who the women were.
Once, just once, I'd like to see your face.

Sometimes mornings, not quite awake,
I stand in front of the mirror rubbing
water into my cheeks. Sometimes I think
my bones are loosening under the skin
and someone else's face is rising in my flesh.
But there is nothing there to betray you—
nothing less, nothing more than blood.

So in the scene they are picking berries:
an old man, two women, the boy.
It is the first time he understands the absence,
the first time a question comes.
It is little more than a stirring behind
a heavy bush, a laugh, a whisper, not
quite a voice, never a face, the wind, no one.

ꗥ *First Snow*

When the air comes sweet
with coal smoke, down
the roof, down the walk,
down a silk of pale trees
between here and the harbor,

my mother shakes the grate
of the big stove, pulls
out a tray of ash as fine
as flour, as white as salt.
Something blossoms under her coat.

The first snow blows in from the sea
and settles like lace
on the black of the yard,
a wind sweeping the white along,
a small wind blowing back a cover.

This is when my great uncle
takes an axe to kindling sticks
and they clink open to
their white bellies, rattling
on the walk like coins.

As the night comes on, he opens
the stove to let me see in.
Blue tongues lick its withered heart
and the air sighs deep and low.
In the night there are always noises.

Heart, belly, lungs, my brother
comes all winter. My mother's disguise
is a bundle of clothes. My stepfather
walks from the wharf each night
with ice on his gloves, salt in his eyes.

When my brother is born, my great uncle takes
to his bed and doesn't notice
the irises rising green and bright,
a small wind licking them
like a mother.

✒ Answering

Nights. The south channel light
winks its eye across the harbor.
It's safe to pass here, it's all right,
all right, in peaceful green,
green star as big as a fist
bringing the boats home over black water.

But you, Mother, you, Brother,
tore your shapes from a paper book
and made the little boats ride on the window sill,
white sill under black glass,
the boats blowing home from your hard lips,
twisting in the dark, in your breath.

This is the seascape of all those dreams,
all those dreams of you and black water
taking us back to you,
all those nights of calling out,
Is it safe to pass? Is it all right?
Those nights of silence and black water answering.

ꟺ Singing to the Dead

Once we saw the moon casting
    its cold rainbow in the blowing spray,
        and then we knew about the dead walking,

how they can be coaxed to rise
    in such light and glow like pearl,
        though they are not concerned with us—

how could they be?
    We huddle in the warm coffins
        of our bodies and hug the rock

that breaks the sea, the rock
    in which they sleep, but they
        are bound by nothing, can float

under the moon, can whisper secrets
    through the damp breast of stone.
        They can tell us what we need to know

and so we sing what we remember:
    Come up, we sing,
        Come out of the rock.

⚓ The Holyoke

The raised iron letters,
those two words stamped in an arc
on that old water-heater in the bathroom,
The Holyoke,
are the first symbols I ever unraveled,
my great-uncle telling me their sound,
pulling the *e* in *The* out long
like the whistle of a teakettle.

The heater didn't work.
We heated our water stovetop
in a copper tub, unremarkable,
but a fact I cling to
as I cling to the quality of light
that seemed always spread
over the tight sidewalk along the house,
a winter gray, old ice, coal ash,
the film over my great-uncle's eye.

When my great-uncle died
his pension stopped coming.
That was the bad time.
Some while after that I got curious.
I opened the arched door
of the old heater
and stared at a helix of coils
thick with dust.
I spent the day there
on the bathroom floor,
measuring my way to the heart of the thing,
turning pipes,
reaming fixtures with an old coathanger.

When I was through, I filled the kerosene bottle
and lighted the wick.
Dusk came on, and that flat light
hung in the square window.
When I opened the faucet, water came,
staccato, brown, warm as flesh.

PART TWO

↙ Catechism

We recite our way to heaven,
obedience, faith, grace, the words
from the blue book in the priest's hands,
our heads turning in the spring light
from his grave eyes to the windows where
yellow birds rise and the lilacs
come swelling up from dark wood.
All things are raised up
in His light, the priest says,
and we after him, *All things
are raised up in His light.*

Down the long hill after,
we cut through Baumgartner's woods
where green already hangs
like satin in the wet air.
We are told a soul lives
in each of us—in me,
in Jaime Duarte, Correro, Santos:
something luminous, yet you cannot
see it, as you cannot see God
the Father but only His works:
ourselves, the earth, the sky.

Santos breaks off, runs
behind a tree, begins a hail
of torn moss. Our school clothes
blossom with smudges. We fire
clods back at him, fan out
along the bog where we come
with strainers in early summer
to scoop black tadpoles from the water.
When we surround the tree

he comes running, trips on a root.
His knees furrow the soft ground.

We roll on him, pin him
to the earth, begin filling
his shirt and pants
with leaves and dirt. He twists
and swears as our hands
rub up into the warmth
under his clothes, feel the damp
grit rough his smooth skin.
He laughs, screams he will fuck us
for this, and then we are all up
and running down the snaking path to town,

Coming out in Baumgartner's yard,
the green junk of an old car,
bottles, wire, his woodpile,
the house lost in a dream of brambles
and wild grapevine. Old man sits
on the porch in his long coat,
curses us, spits on his stair
as we run past, some constant thing
in each of us longing to escape,
glow with grace, our faces
flushing with light when it rises up.

How the Soul Leaves the Body and Finds Its Place in the Presence of God

Only the bravest try it, reaching
out over the highest poles of the trestle,
only at the highest tide, only
when the hoist has stopped
hauling up the heavy buckets for the day.
The rest of us watch from below,
lined on the pilings like skinny gulls.
Then Viegas does it, a leap, the air
shrieks with it, his body falls
in stiff and awkward grace, whacks
into the water by our heels.
We count slowly, watch the foam
until he bursts up, blows water,
shakes his hair into a wreath, the sunlight
blazing white around his face.
He will die the following summer
stealing a Skippy jar full of whisky
and reeling drunk in front of headlights
out on Route Six.
We will see his father grieve
for weeks flying the torn shirt
of his lost boy from the mizzen
of his dragger while the crew
grumbles bad luck.
In catechism the priest says
the soul lives forever, rises up.
His hands are white and soft,
his eyes deep shadows.
We are restless in our metal chairs,
hot, July, a warm tide
swelling in the harbor.

ꙮ *Amazing Grace*

And we learned about Jesus,
how they rolled the stone away
to find him gone, the Holy Ghost,
how sweet the sound of the priest's
quiet words pointing out
something simple about absence
that would take me years to understand.
I cradled my small mother
in my arms once. Once
when she was weeping so openly
and now I can't remember why.
My bones were soft from travel
on water, and I paced the rooms
and no room showed me the way back out.
I felt her shoulders,
how they had grown smaller,
and the soft flesh around them,
and I saw that this was a life
separate from my own, from my memory
of what a life was. Blue flies
gathered on the warm glass of the windows,
buzzed and rose in the oracular light.
When you are living completely in one moment,
you are alive in no other.

Diving for Money

The coin cuts
the air and leaves
its fast trace of light.

You must never move
your eyes from it:
thrash with your hands,
your feet, watch

how it enters among
the grains of sunlight
splashing on the flat water.

The water pushes you up,
the air in your lungs
makes you fly
here in this green world.
You fight to stay down.

Your hair rises like the soft weeds,
your hands cup
in rigid prayer,
your heart falls to your throat
and sings, *Breathe,*

as the thing touches your skin
and your fingers close
around it.

How the surface is like
a perfect sky
when seen from here,
how you rise to it
on your beating legs.

Over and over
it is all there for you,
all you could ever want:

They reach into their pockets
and stars fall around you.
You scoop them from the world
while the quiet longing

comes to you, aching deep
in the lobes of your chest.

✒ Who is Hans Hofmann
and Why Does the World Esteem Him?

So we entered the rooms of the Outsider
   who came each summer with his rent money
      that would buy a family's winter heat,

And someone struck a match
   and then another, but there was nothing
      to steal in this littered place

But canvas and wood and paint
   and tools too strange for any touch
      of ours, except one knife.

Somehow a man's dream
   came forth in green and brutal red,
      opaque squares of yellow, rectangles of blue.

It was something from another world
   and so we stroked it back to ours—
      ribbons and garlands
         and the jagged, blossoming mouths.

~ The Old Town

It was the pheasant place,
brambles and sharp grass
running to the dunes, scoured
with wind. Water rose
in small pools on the bleached sand
where the builders are poised
now with their yellow machines.
It is still a handsome run
for the dark birds. I've heard
their flight, when they burst up,
is fifty miles an hour or more.

I hunted three years, a snot-
nosed boy, and never saw one shot.

My old friend Santos, when
we last talked, leaned over
his beer and said, "I should
have gotten out. There's no leaving now.
You remember those hills? And the way
the sky came down and stuck
in your throat, and all those birds we took?"
Yes, I told him. I told him
how I remembered the cold, the wind,
the gray water, the birds. I hoisted
my glass and drank with him.

And I never took a single bird, ever,
and yes, you should have gotten out.

Stealing Seed Clams from the Marsh

With no light in the sky, I'd feel
my way along the tangled runs
at a dead low tide until
I'd find a bar at first graying
pocked with the tell-tale holes.

I'd rake easy so as not to crush
the fragile shells. They turned
up like corpulent jewels
swathed in their own light, sighed
wetly in the gulf of my hands
as I put them by twos and threes
into the damp and musty burlap.

It was never just for the money
but for the chance of something else,
that sacred hush that we can divine
in anything—as when my cold feet left
glowing prints, white fire sloughing
in the sand behind me, and I thought
only ahead to the warm car, coffee later
at the restaurant where old Howard
would mumble that I'd broken
too many shells again, wink,
give me my seven dollars.

And turning down the last big bend
curving south by a straw-choked flat,
a blind of grass exploded
and the huge bird rose up on wings
long as a man, its black legs trailing,
its neck thrust out, skimming
the bare clumps of grass
out to the shale-dark gray in the west

where it diminished under each
broad beat of wing and left me
shivering, alone on that
silent lip of the earth.

The Old Cellar on Don Sutherland's Property

I go down into the caved-in
hollow like sliding into
another life, like falling
through the cellar door
that burned away with the house
so many years ago. Now leaf
and pine needle and mold
fill the small depression, and
the limbs of the renegade woodlot
clasp above so the light
falls to earth in tatters. Mosquitos
cloud around my face
as I gently dig. The ring
of blackened earth
marks the year of the fire.
I prod with my trowel, my hands,
thinking perhaps a bottle or jar,
or by some miracle a smooth
plate interred unbroken. What
else I can't imagine, except
for the one night on the porch
when I sat sleepless, staring
back at the tumbling stones
of the wall, and out of the dark
tangles of the wood the woman came,
almost nothing, almost mist,
but human yet in the way she moved
to the edge of the light
as if puzzled by this other house,
this heavier world grown up
around her as slowly as the spines
of the huddled trees on that

untended side of the wall.
I believed she might be forming
a question, or that her presence
there was a question, but
too quickly she turned and disappeared,
and on these good days I come
alone to kneel among the ruins
of her house and rummage in soft earth,
wanting to touch something
solid from that buried world,
wondering how I might have answered her,
one who feels so little ease
in his own body.

Crawley's Woods

Fence following dead road, wheel-
ruts grown over with clenched vine,

and you whom I cannot love
lose your way through the deep brush.

I refuse to leave you behind. Long runners
fall from the dense trees; I balance

somehow between the wood and the water:
swamp glow, busy with crawl and flutter,

and in the wet air around us,
the hungry lights of the fireflies.

In these thickets our bodies loosen
and shake out of their lives

like the sudden pickerel jumping
into the world of air

from one of these black pools, his form
shimmering at the edge of spirit

for an impossible moment. Why
do we stand so quietly?

The Woman at the Pond

One summer morning she took
the flowered blouse from her body
and let her long breasts loose
in the sun. The iron water
of the pond said nothing, or perhaps
only hummed softly. We could hear
the *buzz* and *chunk* of living things
all along the shore. Other times
she sat by her easel, quilt of color
patching down the great board she painted.
Could this be our pond? we asked
and held our laughter back among the trees.
When she left each day, we came out
and tracked the soft path down
to her spot by the water's edge.
We laid our gifts there for her,
the sunfish and horned pout we caught
and left to harden in the air.

She sensed our presence more than once.
I remember how her head turned
slowly, her eyes shaded by the broad
brim of her hat, impossible
to tell what moved across her face,
impossible to tell if she forgot
about us as quickly as it seemed,
turning back to her brushes and color,
but I believe that once she worked for us
and drew the town out there where nothing

lay before her but the pond and woods.
Look here, she seemed to say,
See how small your houses are,
how I make their tiny roofs
shrink forever under this
crooked reach of sky.

✦ In the Dunes

And I remember coming in her
for the first time, the surprise
of it that passed through both of us,
the wetness of her mouth and the bright
smell like leaves or cloth that rose
from her breath. So much runs together
now, one summer into another, beach,
dunes, the edge of the scrub woods.
What counts is what is left
to carry off with you.
What counts is that first moment
in which you believe that death
is impossible. You don't ask
yourself or one another where
the dead go, or what it means then
to suffer their absence.
And we shifted our bodies
and I slipped from her, feeling
that small grief. A narrow moon
came up, a crease in the sky, a
curled lip of bare light, and shadows
spread on the hips of the dunes.
I remember how we lay then,
holding each other easily
so neither of us for a time
would move apart from the other,
and then long hushed falling
into the hollow of sleep.

Trying to Remember

You can't tell me a thing
about love, how love stretches
off behind, off in front of you,
two darknesses connected
where they meet by you,
your body that's always looking.

Somehow it all works out.
In a dream I saw my mother
put her life away on the high shelf
of her closet. How odd, I thought,
to see her love lined up like
a set of bone-white dishes.

And my stepfather, too. He
didn't want much and the VA
buried him. I'm not tired
of remembering this. I still dream
and I am always looking
backwards, forwards, you know

how dreams are. Love will
break your bones if you let it.
And yet there is this inviolate
region of light somewhere
at the other edge that we
go traveling off to sometimes,

and it's all there for us,
all the fathers, all their
eyes without tears, and the young
girls who become the mothers,
and there *we* are, of course. This is
what we are trying to remember.

✎ Swing Valley

Oak or elm—I can't see it
clearly anymore, but it was the tallest thing
in that hollow, and someone
always managed to shinny up
to the farthest branch with the end
of a tarred rope to knot there.

Swinging out we moved
from the side of one hill over
the blind rush of bramble
to graze the shoulder of the other bank
and arc back home again.

Summer, winter, summer, of course
those old ropes rotted now and then,
and Carvalho rode one to a parting,
flying down through deep tangles, still
sitting on the knot, his hands clutching
the rope as the bitter end
trailed down like a plume of smoke.

We thought he was all right
when we heard the bushes moving,
and he was. The earth still loved us then,
and the sky watched over us
just as in those stories we heard
about the miracles of the saints,

and a few days later we went up
with another rope, hawked
from the wharf after dark,
and one by one we ran it down,
jumped the knot and swept
across the hollow,

feeling the release and then the pull
of what we already carried with us,
gravity learning the measure
of that unimagined freight.

~ Descent

We dive at the breakwater
when the tide is right,
the currents outbound, the water
low in the deep cuts and channels.
In the murk we hunt eel
and tautog and perch,
holding our breath
with a stitch in our lungs.
Going down I remember
once seeing the other depths,
the outer harbor, over
the side of Carvalho's skiff,
the look of mooring lines
falling off in their perfect curves,
descending, grass-covered,
to where the sunlight weakened
and lay down in a green dusk.
But here the light lies differently
among the deep rocks of the jetty,
and we push into the mottled shadows
and the pressure's heavy hug:
We kick against the current that sends
the long fingers of moss
writhing out from the rocks, in one hand
the spear, homemade and clumsy,
the other hand finding
a nub of rock, holding us still,
breath back, stalking, becoming
the rocks, the streaming weeds,
the fish we've come to turn to prey,
thinking how we could stay here, under,
forget to rise, a kind of sleep,
remembering how Jonah slept

in the belly of a fish, remembering
how we learned to sing into our own ears
to ensure our waking.

PART THREE

Ice Harvest

I know little
about that cutting season
of gray silence
when the men, my mother's
favorite uncle William among them,
walked out on the deep
brindled ice with their long-
handled saws and dark
hooks that curved
like the necks of winter geese,
for my mother was only the girl
in the corner of the photograph,
a thin-faced kid, bundled
in kerchief and coat,
frozen stiff-shouldered,
the look of all the rest
of her life in her eyes.
But I knew the pond
in another time, the old
icehouse a crumbling ruin,
its deep vaults open
to the indifferent sky,
and the bridge like a rib-
cage bleaching, collapsed
in the oily shallows
where the moustached crews
once scored and cut the heavy blocks,
packed them in brown straw
and laid them in the earth:
their ghosts were still learning
the comforts of nothingness—they
never bothered us as we cut
around the blue edges

on our battered skates, our breath
pale shavings in the afternoon sun.
Coming back now it is all gone,
a line of blacktop
curling down a proper lane
of trimmed shrubs, worth going
only so far, to one bend
where a presence comes up, light
lodging in yellow reeds,
and someone's memory—not my own—
of ice in buried darkness whispering
its dissolution, or the even faces
of strangers squinting in the pinched
glow of a dead winter.

ᨓ August

I wanted to show her the dawn
coming up over Truro, I wanted
the sky pulled down
like crepe after a dance.
She wanted me to be Odysseus
and tell her stories of that war
I went off to. She thought
my beard was strange, that I
had been wounded in some deep place
and she wanted to give me something.
August will make you drunk some nights,
gin and touching, the kind of talk
you stumble into, her idea
that two people who are not lovers
can keep something of the world
for themselves, the idea
that something taken from the world
could ever correspond exactly
with what is in any one of us—and more,
that we might recognize this when it happens.

For August the memory is perfect,
the places we touched, the grace
of scattered light drifting
over her cheeks, the runnels
of sand in her black hair,
the way she sucked at the air
after a rush of words,
and then the graying
of the sky down to the east
and the smell of bread as we rapped
on the bakery window

and took hot loaves back to the shore
where a single fishing boat awash in light
pulled a skirt of gulls across the harbor,
its diesel thumping like a heart.

~~~ Limpets

Their lives must be
a kind of sleep, certainly,
since they can know nothing of us,
nor can they know beforehand
the bitter pain of air
or the sun's deadly brightness
or the numbness of chance,

for here at my feet
is the green bottle holding
its cold piece of the sea
and the blind creatures fastened
to their obdurate choice
that last night's wind
heaved up high and dry.

(I remember the wind,
the moon-riding clouds,
dye-blue scud, whip
of the raw northwest, my
head down, walking, hands
buried in pockets, roaming
anywhere in the night
beyond limit and tether,
capable of anything, finding
in this chronic wakefulness
a cold and unfamiliar edge.)

And now by day, the dying breeze,
the lone skiff far out
swinging on a black chain,
a crowd of sea-ducks
sprawling in the old wharf's
ragged lee. A quarter mile down,

a bundled man lets his mastiff
gallop on the sand.
The dog bounds with a force
that reaches across
all this empty sunlight,
and one sharp line in the sky
is dragging the tide away
to someplace as absolute
and as full as yesterday's grave.

The Old Country

My mother would never sweep at night,
would never let us sweep. The broom
rustling, she said, would bring the dead up.
There was a dance to make you shiver
on the kitchen's rotten linoleum.

I saw her cry out once in rage and grief,
pour lighter fluid from the can,
a stream like piss, emptying
her life on the floor. *I'll burn*
this God-damned house down. We never came
from the old country to live like this.

We meant not ourselves but the *os velhos*,
that lean boat from Pico.
My stepfather could not calm her
and found his own rage, knowing somehow
that he had been beaten. He kicked her shins
and refused to weep as we did.

This was a house making its own ghosts.
You learn someday to lie
with your head pressed down,
to roll their old names in your hands,
the cool floor's grit on your cheek,

to call up their old country we only knew
in stories. The voices of the dead
are never what you expect, distant thunder
in the low hills, the dog's howl
at the far end of town, silence.

And this old country is any place
we have to leave. The voices

calling us back are dust.
I have traveled to the far edge
of a country now, fearing the dead.
They still want to speak with my mouth.

Silence

Like a long-legged fly upon a stream
His mind moves upon silence.   —W. B. Yeats

This is his hour to get still, get quiet.
His wife, in her third month,
is in bed with *Middlemarch,*
and he sits downstairs in the kitchen
where the refrigerator's hum breaks off suddenly,
the tail end of its sound sliding out of the house
like a stray piece of moonlight
slipping from the harbor's eye: such silence.
He believes he thinks of nothing now—
the new season's chores are finished,
the roses are pruned,
the garden seeds are in the ground,
the screens in place in the dark,
vine-crowded windows.
There's nothing left for him to do tonight,
nothing for hand or eye to fix upon,
no word or vision needed, no thing to signify,
and yet there is the subtle quaking
that he feels and feels—
no real movement in the frame of the little house
and not the surf shaking the delicate landfill,
but something more like the tension that plays
over the surface of clear, deep pools,
a bourne over which one skates with measured precision
or plunges irrevocably into stranger, dazzling worlds.
In another season he might creep slowly
to the stairs and bed,
hold this woman with their child
building deep in her belly,
but on this night there is no need or hurry.

Summer has come and turned the stars around,
his town prepares its modest sleep,
and he imagines the seabirds at the harbor's edge
poised like statues on the smooth, flat sand.

His Face

His face comes up in dreams sometimes,
a sweet moon blanched of all its poisons,
an artifact I try to bring back with me
pursed in my little hands,

or else he is a dark-hatted dancer
in another dream, a dream of rivers,
tall houses, and birds rising
in pale light above a knot of dancing people.

One night I woke to moonlight
on the bare quilt, moonlight
pinioned on the long walls
as faceless as the dead, and though

he'd lived in me a while, I cupped my hands
and light spilled through like water.

Marriage

Thinking of her now, I watch
the frozen field from our high window,
the way light gathers at the throat
of the dead grass,
the small shapes of the birds
tumbling among the straw
like leaves in the wind,
and this moment so like another
when I sat watching her, the same
absence of sound or touch,
her eyes turning away, moving
off among the black alders
that rose in tangled lines
from their imperfect pools of ice.

Here and there the winter flowers
preen and feather in their hushed places,
the cattails and redberries nod
in the clear temperatures. Her every gesture
each small motion or silence
I can remember
covered whole seasons of our settling,
the locking-in and the thaws
and the long even days without weather,
the going off to walk
where the stripped fingers of the birches
clutch at the last light
and the light rushes off
into the yellow hills.

～ Waking

To leave this dream is bereavement.
Somewhere behind him he's left
the clear ringing of something perfect,
and he cannot breathe a name now
nor conjure a place that does not speak
of some loss. Then he remembers
the girl he saw once in a diner
so many years ago,
a moment incandescent
with the look of her coming in.
Nothing more. A Utah road,
or it was one of those long rolling highways
that run like balm from Denver
into the purple West.

If he could keep the dream it would find her.
It would tumble after her,
though he doesn't know why,
down some narrow road that slips
off past rows of bleached houses,
through endless tracts of field,
sweet onion and puckered grass,
clouds of bright flies
drowning in a long dusk.

But he runs water over his fingers,
his eyes, and sleep falls away
like a brilliant scale:
outside the door is the life
that his life runs to.
And there is still something for him to touch.
A pair of mockingbirds on a black wire

dance out a meaning each to the other,
and this morning's dream becomes their song,
a certain light in the air falling,
falling finally, into his hands.

The World as Will and Idea

The orderlies wheeled our cold brothers
out of that place by the cartloads,
out of the wards and down
the long green tunnels and hallways
to some place I could clearly imagine,
but because my friends knew better
they stole me from my VA bed
and took me home to lie
on a mattress in a yellow room
where my lungs stopped once
when a loud bird screeched in the eaves,
and I flew up to find it.
The heavy thing I left below
wracked the bed and beat for air.

Surprised to be untethered
I remembered oddly as I rose
the lights of the fireflies rising
in the passive dusk of a cornfield,
a roadside where we camped once, a lantern
hissing at the vacant night,
and how in the hospital the rooms
always blackened suddenly at ten,
and the glow from the far stairwell
came sifting through the open doorways.

And then, poised there,
the ineluctable question—
What to do now? Rise forever,
knowing I could rise forever if I wished?
There must be one answer
that goes beyond all this,
the string we dance on

when it is no longer necessary
to separate sunlight, laughter, water,
any one small idea from another.

Out there you can hear
your old flesh crooning—I swear it.
That poor gray fish of self—
its pain was what I swam on
until by perfect choice I fell
back into the world, those other lights,
the ponderous lights of the body,
singing me home for a while.

✺ Catwalk

To fall from the bow catwalk
was certain death, and so nights
it was off limits,
and so nights we'd go there
between launch and recovery
and lie on the wire mesh,
pass a joint, watch the stars,
the white bone of the bow-wave
stories beneath us.

The shore bristled
with our gifts of light,
and there was white bone
in the sky, too, splitting
it down the middle.

Then we heard the story of the sailor
on another carrier
who rolled from a gun-tub
and swam all the black night
until a tin can found him
in the impossible dawn.

Sometimes a terror came over you.
Something you couldn't name—worse
than the idea of falling
into night forever, something
to hold you, knuckles cramped
on the steel net, seeing
the beast you rode for what it was,

knowing that the thrumming you heard
in the dark chambers below decks
was a heart beating like your own,
and then the dreams
that you'd somehow already fallen.

Carmelita Raez

My face is the face
just behind hers, my arms
come around her at the waist.
She holds my clasped
hands in her own
and stares at the camera.
This is downstairs.
The bar is drunk with sailors
hugging their girls.
Everyone is young,
but she is old enough
to have one kid, gone
to Manila now with a sister,
she told me in better English
than the other girls spoke
although when she swore she broke
into Tagalog, sometimes Spanish.
She still wore her ring
from the Catholic Girls' School,
red stone, I'm no whore.

Upstairs in the monkeywood
bed, she held me when
I couldn't stop shaking,
told me how she swam
for coins in the shit river
until her breasts came,
drank San Miguel with me
all night, calling the boy
for fried eggs and noodles.
Days we flitted in jitneys
down the squat streets,
off limits. I gave her rolls

of strange money, she took
care of everything, could
butterfly the blade
of her knife open
in the space of a heartbeat:
Stay, she said, I'll hide you,
don't go back, you live
with me, we'll make
love all the time,
buy me soap, buy
me perfume. We
washed in the square
at the public pump, her
brown hand like something
out of the *selva*
brushing my skin.

Smoke is what I remember now,
its ripe stink from the shacks—
and dogs, the naked kids,
an open radio, its viscera glowing
rock and roll from the Armed
Forces station. On the mud
road to the beach, my last day,
screen of leaves swallowing us,
she pulled off her shirt
to show me the scar I'd only
seen in the dark,
told me how she cut the man
who gave it to her. Someday,
she said, the old headhunters
will come back out of the jungle
and eat up this town. Not me.
I'll be somewhere else. Kiss
my shoulders, kiss my cheeks.

Later, back on the line,
the watches running four and four
and the choppers whacking
at the edge of the world,
her blue envelope, the photograph
I still find and find again, each
year a little darker
at the silvered edges, and in
her neat and careful hand:
Send me love from far away,
send me cigarettes and lotion,
something pretty to wear in my hair
on the nights I go out dancing.

The Bullet Hole in the Twelfth-Street Door

It sprawls from the perfect circle
at its center like a star spreading
in the thick glass of the door.
Sight along it and it frames the shabby street
with its surprised mouth, a constant O
of quiet rage, outrage, the arbitrary
punctuation hurled from the alley or
the heavy-throated passing car
on a lightless morning.

But now sunlight issues through
this webbed fissure, the lean street
is raked with the groan of buses,
the students pass up and down the tiled halls
bathed in weary light.
A star, then, yes. A hole in
the fabric, the firmament, the random
message from another world,
light years beyond, the other side.

Listen and the world hisses
at the crystal bruise.
What's to become of us?
Who are these aliens at the gates?
The curriculum ticks away
like an immense clock
and does not answer, for it is possible
that the world is mind, and therefore
all worlds might balance
precariously on a single thought.
It is time for classes to begin.

Perhaps we are close now
to a great and final revelation

as the posters on the kiosk tell us
in smug Roman letters, but just now
see how the city pushes its common light
upon the glass, the dazzling spider
projected yellow on the far wall
above the gathered heads.

⚜ Passing

Today on my front lawn
four young girls stop without seeing me
to shout and play
in some small interruption
of their passing down the street.
Two of them already have small breasts
beneath their shirts, mild buds
they do not seem to care about
or even want this afternoon.
They stop to do cartwheels on my grass.
The tallest one, in a skirt, looks down
the sidewalk and seeing no one
tumbles, all legs and underpants.
When she whirls, she breaks
the daylight apart, and her friends
find that they must shriek
in this much joy. They somersault
until they make the green earth spin,
but this older one, their leader, this plain
girl who holds her face grave, distant
as some heavenly body, eyes fixed
on some far-off point the others
cannot see, cartwheels
into an awkward split, the sunlight
showing through to the small dark hand
blossoming beneath her pink nylon.
She rolls to her round knees.
In a moment something passes over her face:
It is like the light she has found here
in the dapples on the grass, and she
skips away with it as the others
skip behind. But scarcely past

71

the white driveway she slows,
walks, and this light leaves her
and comes fluttering back to my lawn,
left flattened now from the simple
crush of their small bodies.

February, The Moors

Although I'll never know this marsh entirely,
all that assembles under the ice
of this winter moon, the reaches
where the mud heaves the methane up,
its warrens of reeds, the whistle
of the wild ducks beating down
the long curve out to sea,

I can return here
and believe I understand something else,
something about journey and distance,
how on that other coast, in my wife's belly
a stranger is called forth and moves,
nameless yet, through water and darkness.

This is how it must be simply:

Because I loved a person in a certain way,
    nothing happened;

or because I loved a person in a certain way,
    someone fell from sleep, far off.

And there is Venus rising in the night
and scattering in the wind-ruff on the tide.
And the other stars I know
and the stars I can't name

are lying down on the water
in cold ribbons of light
simply because they do.

November, California

The fence wire is dying of rust
and anyway it cannot keep back
the slide of brush from the brown hills.
Huge creatures lumbered here once,
lowed their song under the tin roofs
of the open barns, all empty now
except for the rows of corroding lockers
and one plow, utterly ruined.
Now we walk here from the house
to listen for the owl
or to watch the moon slip
like ice through the stars.

My son, in the pack on my stomach,
stirs and makes his small
womb-sounds. He knows I'm not
his mother, but I'll suffice for now,
just as the clear night rising
through the bent forms of the oak trees
is all we have of something else.
If I look hard I can see a pale
flare of light from the warm house;
if I wait long enough perhaps
a swooping shadow,
maybe the loud rush of wings.

The Resting Place

Small dark pines rise near it,
down by the bogs where black birds
rush up on orange wing. I'm told
that a farmhouse stood once
at the edge of the sandhills,
and there were wheel ruts running
as far away as another lifetime.

But it is foolish to think of travel
beyond these fingers of light and darkness,
for what you leave behind calls after you—
the wing of the black cricket,
the frog's throat in harsh choir,
the mute dance of thistle shaking
against the plain beachgrass.

Yet there is no fortune good enough
to let you return, to sleep forever
in this one place, its heavy iron gate
scaled with rust, its postpile of stones
pitched crazy by the frost-heaves,
lost for years now in the clutch
of the knotted briar and green moss
that run to the marsh's quiet edge.

🌿 Joshua Trees

One night with the wind
blowing down from the high canyons
we wrapped ourselves in scarves and hoods
and I took her up the dry wash
between creosote and boulder
to see the flame of coyote
in the long winter shadows.

The wind numbed our fingers
and slowed the blue stars
in their tracks. Each bush
rattled. The watchers
were being watched. Everything
turned light or shadow, our shapes
dissolving in the arms of the Joshua trees,

and overhead in the sparse heaven
one errant trace, a tumbling
satellite scratching its wing
on the Pleiades. All around us
in the frozen desert nervous eyes
burned wild with grace as those
splayed lilies rose shouting.

Old Bones, Breakwater

This is where the old ship-bones come down, finally,
come blackening and softening, trailing
seaweed and sea grass: ribs that the small
crabs burrow under, that the barnacles
latch to, that the mussels hold onto
in their clusters of long blue grapes. I know
it's the tide and wind that pull boats here
to rest in death against the cold granite
of the sea wall, but I can't help
seeing it all another way, the sunken
hulks drawing themselves across the sandy bottom,
the clam-pocked flats, the eel-grass,
walking—if boats ever walked—the ghostwalk
of the newly dead. I remember
on the hard bright days one winter,
in the year my stepfather came with his shovel
to join the repair crews along that mile of dike,
lucky for the work, plying stone to stone
along the deep wall's bottom, when I would visit
with soup for him in a thermos
or a fresh pack of Pall Malls from my mother.
I'd dodge that razor wind by walking
low along the stone shoulders,
make my way farther out than the workers
and settle above one of those decaying wrecks,
in any one of them the likeness of a fish or animal
or man, the hollow in the belly, the bend
of the long keel spine. I can find one
there yet—one or another—and let
my memory run to it: They die and continue
dying, renounce something of themselves
with each new tide, take on more
of their disappearance under the beak of worm

and bore of shell, so that what remains
is only a brace of arms thrown up
as if to hug the currents of their own unraveling,
as though this long effacement were like memory itself,
lessening, lightening, moving back across the elements
where the final giving up of shape lies half-buried,
perhaps the one secret of what we know as healing.

ᔐ Golden Colt Ranch

We never got as far as Mexico,
our dream of saffron cliffs
and maguey running to the blue Gulf,
but here in the chaparral hills
over our arid valley
there is little difference—*aguacate*
greens the steps above our ruin
of a house. The arroyo is dry. The dry
frogs shriek at a lake of stars.
I remember how Jaime Duarte
told us once in catechism
that he'd seen Jesus floating
in the dark sky, a soft light
above his house. The priest
kept him after class for a long time.
That's all there was to it.
Sometimes a coyote
yips in the high brush,
sometimes a light in the sky
shivers, breaks, dies hissing.
Down in the live oak stand
there are cool piles of leaves
to lie on, and Christ's peace
seems as plausible as bread
or water or starlight, so
we lie down in the shadows waiting
in the darkness to be filled.

A NOTE ON THE AUTHOR

Born and raised in Provincetown, Massachusetts, Frank Gaspar now lives in southern California with his wife and son. He has been a Bread Loaf Scholar and received a California Arts Commission Scholarship to the Squaw Valley Community of Writers. His poems have appeared in *The Kenyon Review*, *The Georgia Review*, *The Nation*, *Prairie Schooner*, *The Massachusetts Review*, *The New England Review and Bread Loaf Quarterly*, and other literary journals.

A NOTE ON THE PRIZE

The Samuel French Morse Poetry Prize was established in 1983 by the Northeastern University Department of English in order to honor Professor Morse's distinguished career as teacher, scholar, and poet. Professor Morse died on May 13, 1985. The members of the prize committee are Francis C. Blessington, Joseph deRoche, Victor Howes, Stuart Peterfreund, and Guy Rotella.